Oct07-DPA(

DISCARD

DATE DUE			

DEMCO 38-297

CRIME Solvers

Terrorist FILE
The Lockerbie Investigation

by Amanda Howard

Consultant: Dr. John P. Cassella
Principal Lecturer in Forensic Science
Staffordshire University, England

BEARPORT
PUBLISHING

New York, New York

Credits

Cover, © Tom Kidd/Alamy, © Stephen Strathdee/Shutterstock, © Jurgen Ziewe/ Shutterstock, and © Rex Features; Title Page, © Rex Features; 4, © Aviation-images. com; 5T, © Rex Features; 5B, © Rex Features/Action Press; 6, © Rex Features/Bryn Colton; 7, © Rex Features; 8L, © Rex Features/I.T.N; 8R, © Rex Features/Sipa Press; 9, © Ticktock Media Archive; 10, © Rex Features/Tom Kidd; 11T, © Rex Features; 11B, © Ron Sachs/CNP/Corbis; 12, © Shutterstock; 13T, © Shutterstock; 14, © Crown Office and Procurator Fiscal Service; 15L, © Rex Features/Tom Kidd; 15R, © Shutterstock; 16, © Crown Office and Procurator Fiscal Service; 17T, © Crown Office and Procurator Fiscal Service; 17B, © Crown Office and Procurator Fiscal Service; 18, © Crown Office and Procurator Fiscal Service; 19L, © Rex Features/Peter MacDiarmid; 19R, © Crown Office and Procurator Fiscal Service; 20L, © Crown Office and Procurator Fiscal Service; 20R, © Rex Features; 21L, © Crown Office and Procurator Fiscal Service; 21R, © Crown Office and Procurator Fiscal Service; 22L, © Crown Office and Procurator Fiscal Service; 22R, © Crown Office and Procurator Fiscal Service; 24, © Rex Features/ Sipa Press; 25T, © Rex Features/Sipa Press; 25B, © Rex Features/Action Press; 28, © Ron Sachs/CNP/Corbis; 29T, © Shutterstock; 29B, © Science Photo Library/Michel Viard/Peter Arnold Inc; 30, © Rex Features/Sipa Press.

Every effort has been made by ticktock Entertainment Ltd. to trace copyright holders. We apologize in advance for any omissions. We would be pleased to insert the appropriate acknowledgments in any subsequent edition of this publication.

Publisher: Kenn Goin
Editorial Director: Adam Siegel
Project Editor: Dinah Dunn
Creative Director: Spencer Brinker
Original Design: ticktock Entertainment Ltd.

Library of Congress Cataloging-in-Publication Data

Howard, Amanda, 1973-
  Terrorist file : the Lockerbie investigation / by Amanda Howard.
    p. cm. — (Crime solvers)
  Includes bibliographical references and index.
  ISBN-13: 978-1-59716-552-5 (library binding)
  ISBN-10: 1-59716-552-2 (library binding)
 1. Pan Am Flight 103 Bombing Incident, 1988—Juvenile literature. 2. Terrorism—United States—Juvenile literature. 3. Terrorism—Europe—Juvenile literature. 4. Bombing investigation—Scotland—Lockerbie—Juvenile literature. I. Title.

  HV6431.H6923 2008
  363.12'465094147—dc22
                                    2007016520

Contents

Flight 103's Last Moments

Pan Am Flight 103 took off at 6:25 P.M. from London's Heathrow Airport on December 21, 1988. It was an ordinary flight on a cloudless day.

The 747 flew over Scotland on its way to New York. No one on board had any idea the plane would never reach its destination.

Alan Topp, an **air traffic controller** at Scotland's Prestwick Airport, followed the plane's flight path on his **radar** screen. At 7:02 P.M., the plane suddenly disappeared from Alan's screen. He tried to radio the captain, but there was no response.

Alan looked back at his radar screen. Something was wrong. Where the plane had been, there were now several objects moving quickly apart. Pan Am Flight 103 had exploded!

An air traffic controller watches the movements of planes on his computer.

FACT FILE

Air Traffic Controller

- Air traffic controllers keep track of planes flying across land and sea.

- They use radar to monitor many planes at one time.

- Air traffic controllers give directions to planes to make sure that they don't crash.

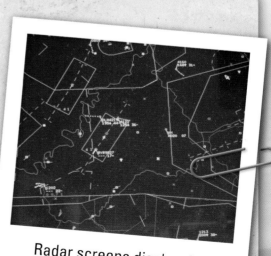

Radar screens display the positions of planes in flight.

The Explosion

The plane was flying at 31,000 feet (9,449 m) when its front **luggage hold** exploded, leaving a hole. Air rushing into the hole caused the plane to tear apart.

Many of the 259 people on board were killed instantly. The rest died 46 seconds later when the plane hit the ground.

The nose of the Boeing 747, named *Maid of the Seas*, after it hit the ground

The wind scattered **victims** and **debris** over 845 square miles (2,189 sq km) in Scotland and England. Most of the plane crashed into the small Scottish farming town of Lockerbie.

A huge wing section containing 200,000 pounds (90,718 kg) of fuel smashed into one neighborhood. The ground shook when the wing hit. A fireball shot 300 feet (91 m) into the air. Eleven people on the ground were killed in the blaze.

The plane's wings and fuel hit this neighborhood in Lockerbie. It created a fireball that destroyed five homes.

FACT FILE

The Flight

Plane:	Airline:	Pilot:	Maximum speed:
Boeing 747-121	Pan Am (Pan American World Airways)	Captain James MacQuarrie	636 miles per hour (1,024 kph)

Explosion over Lockerbie, Scotland

Atlantic Ocean

London, England

New York, U.S.A.

The planned route of Flight 103 from London to New York

Crash Down in Lockerbie

The town of Lockerbie looked like a war zone. Baggage and bodies had rained down for miles. There were piles of crumpled steel everywhere. A jet engine the size of a small truck landed near an apartment building.

Jasmine Bell, who lived in Lockerbie, said "fire was falling down from the sky." She had been so frightened she couldn't move.

A house on fire in Lockerbie

One of the engines from the plane crashed in Lockerbie's town center.

Soon after the crash, police and firefighters from nearby towns raced to the scene. **Investigators** from the Army, Royal Air Force, and British government arrived soon after. Since 189 Americans had died on the plane, the United States' **FBI** and **CIA** also joined the investigation. They all wanted to answer the same question. Was the explosion a tragic accident or was it caused by a bomb?

FACT FILE

How the Plane Blew Apart

- An explosion in the front luggage hold caused the **nose cone** and **cockpit** to tear apart from the plane.

- The front section of the plane crashed in a field three miles (4.8 km) from Lockerbie.

- The **fuselage** and wings of the plane traveled 13 miles (21 km) through the air. They broke into smaller pieces before hitting the ground.

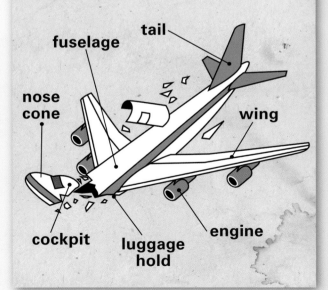

fuselage

tail

nose cone

wing

cockpit

luggage hold

engine

The Investigation

More than 2,000 people searched Lockerbie and the surrounding countryside for debris from the crash. They hoped to find clues about what caused the plane to explode.

The searchers worked in groups of eight or ten. They tagged each piece of debris and noted its location. Then each piece was moved to a local school's gym.

Experts used chemicals to search for signs of **explosives**. More than three million pieces of **evidence** and almost 90 percent of the aircraft were eventually recovered.

Police searching a large area around the crash site for clues

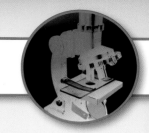

The **flight data recorder** was found within 24 hours of the explosion. It is also called the "black box." This machine records conversations in the cockpit. Investigators listened to the recorder, but found no evidence of a call for help.

Investigators carefully examined evidence found in the search.

FACT FILE
Straight Line Searching

- The investigators hunted for clues using a method called "straight line searching." They walked shoulder-to-shoulder, looking up and down and from side to side.

- Searchers at Lockerbie were given a simple instruction, "If it isn't growing and it isn't a rock, pick it up."

- Investigators were most interested in finding items that were burned. Hopefully, these items could provide clues as to whether a bomb had exploded.

Investigators walk side-by-side when using the straight line method.

Body Identification

Investigators also began the sad task of **identifying** the bodies. This was difficult because the faces of many victims were damaged in the crash. **Forensic** dentists were called in to help. They were trained to identify victims by looking at their teeth.

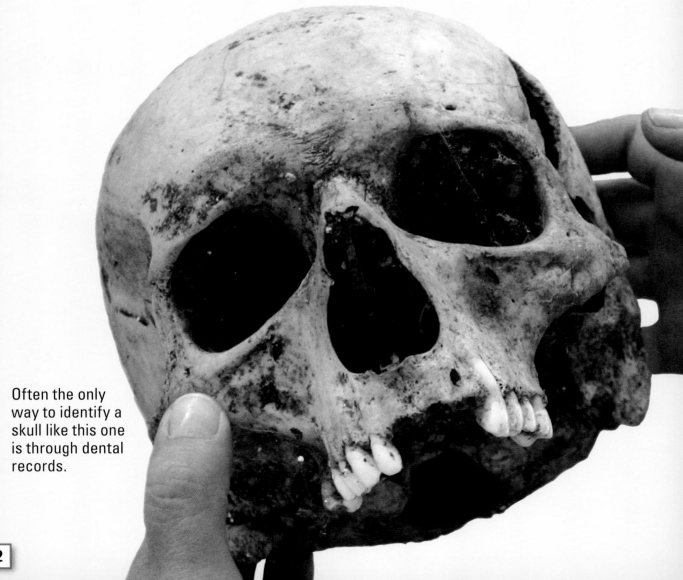

Often the only way to identify a skull like this one is through dental records.

Investigators hoped to learn more about the cause of the crash by studying the victims. When a body was found, they recorded its location and any nearby wreckage.

After a body was identified, investigators checked to see where the person was sitting on the plane. This information helped them figure out where on the plane the explosion occured.

FACT FILE
Forensic Dentists

- Forensic dentists help identify dead bodies when the victims' faces are unrecognizable.

- They note the shape and position of the teeth. They also note anything unusual, such as fillings or braces. Such items are compared to old X-rays or dental records of the victim.

- If there are no dental records, a victim's photograph is compared to the teeth to see if they are the same.

- Forensic dentists can sometimes identify a person from a single tooth.

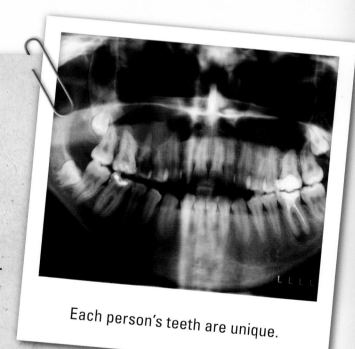

Each person's teeth are unique.

The Bomb

Investigators put the pieces of the plane together like a jigsaw puzzle. They found a 20-inch (50.8-cm) hole on the lower left side, near the luggage hold. Scientists examined the area around the hole and found traces of explosives.

In the debris, they found pieces of a Toshiba BomBeat cassette player, clothing, and an umbrella. All were burned and had tiny bits of explosive material on them. They also found a piece of an MST-13 timer. This machine is used to set off explosions. Investigators now knew they were looking for a bomb.

A Toshiba cassette player like this one was used in the bombing.

In July 1990, investigators determined what caused the explosion. A bomb made from plastic explosives was hidden inside a cassette player. The cassette player was wrapped in clothing and placed in a suitcase with an umbrella. Investigators had the clues they needed to locate the bomber.

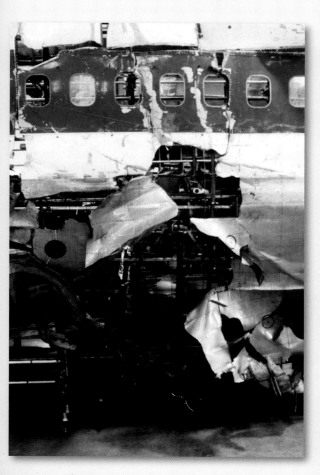

Investigators slowly rebuilt the plane, piece by piece.

FACT FILE
Explosives

- There are two types of explosives.

- *Low explosives:* They explode by burning quickly and are usually started by a flame. They are not as dangerous as high explosives. Gun powder is a low explosive.

- *High explosives:* They explode more violently than low explosives. They are used to make weapons and to knock down buildings. Flight 103 was destroyed by high explosives.

Dynamite is a high explosive.

The Evidence

Investigators determined that the explosive used in Flight 103 was Semtex. This information led them to Libya. The country had recently bought 1,000 tons (907,185 kg) of this explosive. The Libyan government had also purchased a number of the MST-13 timers that set off the explosion.

This picture shows how explosives were hidden inside the cassette player.

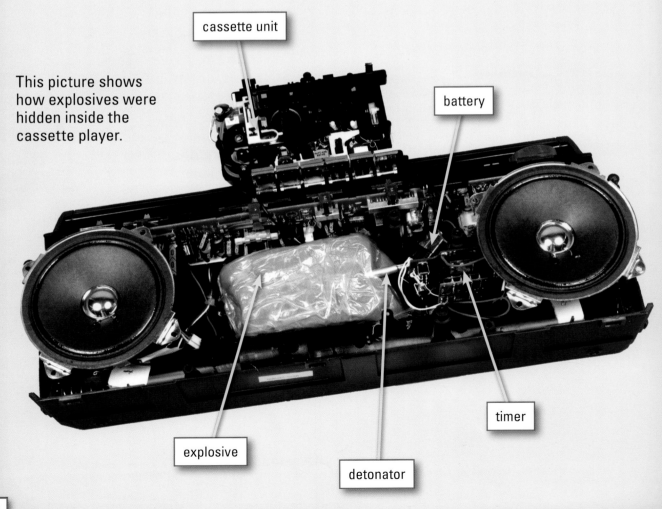

cassette unit

battery

explosive

detonator

timer

Libya felt they had a reason to want to hurt Americans. In 1986, **terrorists** had blown up a disco in Berlin, Germany. Two U.S. soldiers were killed and more than 200 people were injured. Many of these were Americans.

The United States responded by bombing the terrorists' training camps in Libya. News reports said Libya's leader had been injured and his daughter killed in the U.S. attack. Some say the bombing of Flight 103 was Libya's way of getting back at America.

The hole in the luggage hold, caused by the bomb

FACT FILE

Semtex

- The bomb in Pan Am Flight 103 was made of a powerful plastic explosive called Semtex.

- Plastic explosives are soft and can be shaped by hand. This makes them easy to hide in other containers.

- Airport X-ray machines can not detect Semtex.

Blocks of Semtex

The Trail Leads to Malta

Investigators had found scraps of clothes that had been packed with the bomb. They were labeled "Yorkie" and "Made in Malta." These were important clues.

Investigators found out which shops sold Yorkie clothing. This led them to a store called Mary's House in Malta, a country north of Libya. Its owner, Tony Gauci, remembered the customer who bought the clothes. He provided a description, which an artist turned into a drawing.

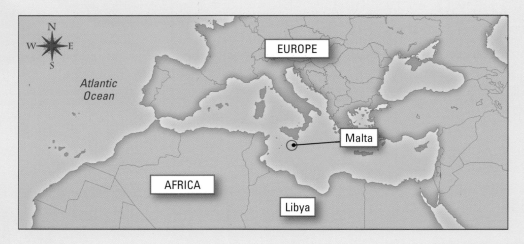

Artists created this sketch (left) and photo (right) based on the description given to investigators by the owner of Mary's House.

Investigators now had an idea of what the bomber looked like. They began searching for Libyans living in Malta. They were getting closer to finding a **suspect**.

The bomber bought a number of items at this shop in Malta.

This clothing label led the investigators to the store in Malta that sold Yorkie clothing.

The Suspects

The evidence gathered by investigators led them to two suspects. Abdelbaset Ali Mohmed al-Megrahi was identified as the man who had purchased the clothing at Mary's House. He was an officer in the Libyan government and head of security at Libyan Arab Airlines. He was also involved in the purchase of the MST-13 timers for the Libyan government.

The other suspect was Al Amin Khalifa Fhimah. He was an employee of Libyan Arab Airlines in Malta. Investigators thought he had helped al-Megrahi get the bomb onto the plane.

Abdelbaset Ali Mohmed al-Megrahi

Al Amin Khalifa Fhimah

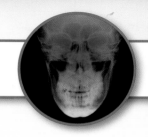

In 1991, **warrants** were issued for the arrest of the two men. Libya's government wanted to know where the suspects would be tried before they would release them. A Scottish court in the Netherlands was determined to be a fair place to hold the trial. In 1999, the men were flown from Libya to the Netherlands to stand trial for killing 270 people.

The Timing Device That Led to al-Megrahi

- A tiny piece of a circuit board was found in the wreckage at Lockerbie.

- It was identified as part of an MST-13 timer, which was made by MEBO Electronics.

- MEBO claimed that al-Megrahi was the man who had received the MST-13 timers for Libya in the 1980s.

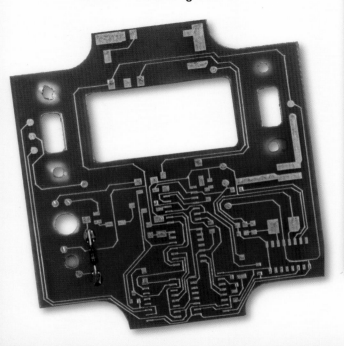

A complete circuit board from an MST-13 timing device

A broken piece of the circuit board

The Plan

Investigators used the evidence they found to piece together al-Megrahi's movements before the disaster. Two weeks before the bombing, al-Megrahi hid the bomb in a cassette player and put it in a suitcase. He then flew from Malta to Frankfurt, Germany.

When al-Megrahi arrived at Frankfurt, he sent the suitcase on to London. The suitcase had fake airline tags. These allowed it to be put on board when al-Magrahi was not on the plane. Fhimah worked at the airport in Malta at the time of the bombing. Investigators believe he provided these tags. The suitcase arrived at Heathrow Airport in London. The fake tags allowed it to be put on the plane to New York.

Investigators made a reconstruction of the suitcase containing the bomb.

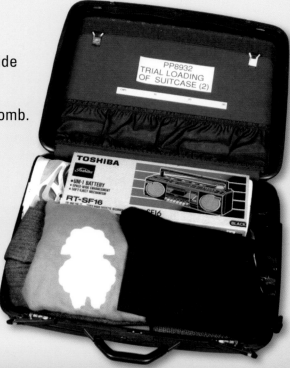

Fhimah's ID for the Malta airport

The bomb inside the suitcase was timed to explode over the Atlantic Ocean. Al-Megrahi hoped any evidence would be lost deep in the water. He did not know that the flight's take-off would be delayed 25 minutes. This delay was the reason the plane exploded over Lockerbie instead of the ocean.

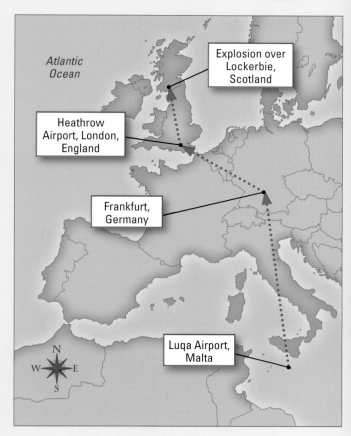

This map shows the journey of the suitcase with the bomb inside.

FACT FILE

An Early Warning?

- On December 5, 1988, a man with an Arabic accent called the American Embassy in Finland.

- He said that a Pan Am flight from Frankfurt to the United States would be blown up in the next two weeks.

- The threat was taken seriously. Security was increased at many airports in Europe, though not at Frankfurt. The warning about the threat was found under a pile of papers the day after the bombing.

The Trial

The trial of Abdelbaset Ali Mohmed al-Megrahi and Al Amin Khalifa Fhimah began in May 2000. Both men were charged with killing 270 people— 259 on the plane and 11 in Lockerbie.

The trial lasted for nearly a year and cost approximately $90 million. On January 31, 2001, al-Megrahi was found guilty of murder. He was sentenced to 27 years in prison. His suspected partner, Al Amin Khalifa Fhimah, was found not guilty. Investigators did not prove beyond a reasonable doubt that he was involved.

A Libyan policeman (left) taking al-Megrahi to trial

In August 2003, Libya accepted responsibility for the Lockerbie bombing. It agreed to pay a **settlement** of about $10 million to each of the victim's families. The investigators had solved the crime and brought the terrorists to justice.

Yet for the victims' families and friends, the tragedy would never be forgotten. Kara Weipz, who lost her brother in the bombing, said, "No settlement will ever take away our grief or anger."

Fhimah (left) with Libyan police officers

FACT FILE

Witnesses at the Trial

The statements of **witnesses** helped prove that al-Megrahi was guilty. These included:

- MEBO employees, who said they had sold al-Megrahi timing devices for bombs.

- The owner of the shop, Mary's House, who recognized al-Megrahi as the man who had bought the clothes that were wrapped around the bomb.

Five judges at the Lockerbie trial

Case Closed

December 5, 1988

A caller warns the American Embassy in Finland that in the next two weeks a bomb will be placed on a Pan Am flight to New York.

December 21, 1988

6:25 P.M. Pan Am Flight 103 to New York takes off 25 minutes late from London's Heathrow Airport.

7:02 P.M. The plane explodes over the town of Lockerbie, Scotland. All 259 people on board die, as well as 11 people on the ground.

1988–1989

- Investigators try to figure out the cause of the plane crash. Searchers gather millions of pieces of evidence.

- On December 28, 1988, investigators find signs of the explosives that caused the crash.

- Scraps of clothing and fragments of a suitcase and cassette player are found.

- A fragment of the MST-13 timer for the bomb is found. This helps link the bomb to Libya and Abdelbaset Ali Mohmed al-Megrahi.

August 1989

Investigators locate the shop in Malta where the clothing that was wrapped around the bomb was purchased. The shop owner gives police a description of the Libyan man who bought the clothes, later identified as Abdelbaset Ali Mohmed al-Megrahi.

November 12, 1991

Warrants are issued for the arrests of al-Megrahi and Fhimah.

May 23, 2000

The trial of al-Megrahi and Fhimah begins in the Netherlands.

January 31, 2001

Al-Megrahi is found guilty of murder and sentenced to 27 years in prison. Fhimah is found not guilty.

August 2003

Libya accepts responsibility for the Lockerbie bombing. It agrees to pay each of the victim's families about $10 million.

Crime Solving Up Close

Forensic Search Techniques

Investigators in Lockerbie had a lot of help finding evidence, including:

- *Search teams* — who examine a **crime scene** for objects that investigators can use to help solve a case.

- *Photographers* — who take pictures of the evidence and the crime scene.

- *Evidence recorders* — who write down detailed information about where and how evidence is found.

Searchers collect evidence in a number of ways:

Straight line search:
People in a search party walk side-by-side in a straight line, looking for anything unusual. If something is found, the entire line stops while the evidence is collected. This method was used at Lockerbie.

Spiral search:
The search begins in a small circle around the main crime scene. It continues in larger circles until the whole crime scene is covered.

Strip search:
This method is used when a small number of people must search a large area. They cover it in straight lines, walking back and forth.

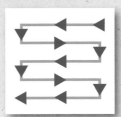

Grid searches:
The crime scene is divided into small squares. Searchers then examine each square before moving to the next one.

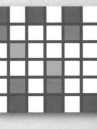

Collecting Evidence from a Bomb

Finding evidence after a bomb explodes is a huge task. In Lockerbie, searchers had to cover 845 square miles (2,189 sq km) of Scotland and England.

They were most interested in finding items that may have been pieces of the bomb. These items could include:

- batteries
- wires
- detonators
- timers
- cell phones
- ball bearings
- nails
- duct tape

Injuries on victims, both dead and alive, are checked closely. Are explosive powders, burns, or pieces of a bomb present on the victim? If so, they can provide clues.

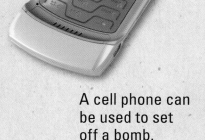

A cell phone can be used to set off a bomb.

A forensic scientist checks an object for signs of explosives.

Every piece of wreckage is X-rayed and examined for evidence of explosives. It can provide experts with details such as the number or type of explosives used, and where a bomb was placed.

Crime Solving Up Close

Air Crash Investigation

Air crash investigators try to learn everything that happened to a plane before it crashed.

- The first thing investigators look for is the flight data recorder or "black box." It records what pilots say and stores information from instruments in the cockpit. These recordings can show what happened before the crash. For example, pilots might be heard talking about problems such as engine failure.

- Major pieces of wreckage are looked at first. If they are far apart, it is proof that the plane blew apart before hitting the ground.

- In cases like Pan Am Flight 103, the pieces of the plane are put together like a jigsaw puzzle. Any damage or holes show investigators where the bomb was located.

Black boxes are actually orange. Their bright color helps investigators find them at a crash site.

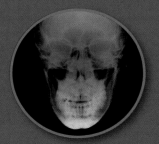

Glossary

air traffic controller (AIR TRAF-ik kuhn-TROHL-ur) a person who gives directions to planes, prevents collisions, and helps plane traffic move safely around airports

CIA (SEE EYE AY) abbreviation for Central Intelligence Agency; an organization that gathers information in foreign countries for the U.S. government

cockpit (KOK-*pit*) the area in the front of the plane where the pilot sits

crime scene (KRIME SEEN) an area where an illegal act has taken place

debris (duh-BREE) scattered pieces of something that has been destroyed

evidence (EV-uh-duhnss) objects and information that help prove something happened

explosives (ek-SPLOH-sivz) substances that can blow up

FBI (EF BEE EYE) abbreviation for Federal Bureau of Investigation; an organization that looks into crimes for the U.S. Department of Justice

flight data recorder (FLITE DAY-tuh ri-KOR-dur) a machine that stores information about a plane's journey

forensic (fuh-REN-sik) using science and technology to help solve crimes

fuselage (FYOO-suh-lahzh) the main body of the plane

identifying (eye-DEN-tuh-*fye*-ing) telling who someone is or what something is

investigators (in-VESS-tuh-*gate*-urz) detectives

luggage hold (LUGH-ij HOHLD) the place on a plane where suitcases are stored

nose cone (NOHZ KOHN) the pointed front part of a plane

radar (RAY-dar) a system that finds solid objects by bouncing radio waves off of them

settlement (SET-uhl-muhnt) the final payment

suspect (SUHSS-pekt) a person who is thought to have committed a crime

terrorists (TER-ur-ists) people who use violence to get what they want

victims (VIK-tuhmz) people who are hurt or killed

warrants (WOR-uhnts) legal papers that allow officers to carry out the law

witnesses (WIT-niss-ez) people who describe the scene they saw

Index

Read More

Dahl, Michael, and Barbara B. Rollins. *Cause of Death.* Mankato, MN: Capstone Press (2004).

Spies, Karen Bornemann. *Pan Am Flight 103: Terrorism Over Lockerbie.* Berkeley Heights, NJ: Enslow Publishers, Inc. (2003).

Wicker, R. Doug. *The Bombing of Pan Am Flight 103.* New York: The Rosen Publishing Group, Inc. (2003).

Learn More Online

To learn more about crime solving and the Lockerbie investigation, visit **www.bearportpublishing.com/CrimeSolvers**

About the Author

Amanda Howard writes extensively about true crime, including the encyclopedia *River of Blood: Serial Killers and Their Victims*. She is currently studying for her Bachelor of Social Science in Criminology, Criminal Law and Psychology. She lives near Sydney, Australia with her family.